The Mystery Message

by Carter W. Ryan
illustrated by Angela Adams

HOUGHTON MIFFLIN   BOSTON

Printed in China

ISBN 10: 0-618-90004-7
ISBN 13: 978-0-618-90004-6

23456789 NOR 16 15 14 13 12 11 10 09 08

"I won!" shouted Hector, waving a postcard.

"What did you win?" asked his twin sister, Isabella.

"Last month I found a contest in one of my magazines. I had to figure out a secret code," Hector explained. "First prize was two tickets to the Acme Toy Company. I figured out the secret code, and I won the tickets!"

"Wow," said Isabella. She looked disappointed.

"What's wrong, Izzy?" Hector asked with a smile. "Don't you want to go with me?"

"Really? You'd let me have one of the tickets? Oh, thank you!" She hugged her brother.

Mr. Vega, Hector and Isabella's father, agreed to take them to the factory. The next Saturday at 9:00, Hector, Isabella, and Mr. Vega piled into the car. They buckled their seat belts and were on their way!

Half an hour later, they pulled up in front of the Acme Toy Company. Huge gates surrounded the building. A flag flew at the top of each corner of the building. The four flags were bright red with the letters ATC in blue in the middle. "Acme Toy Company," murmured Hector. "I can't believe we're here!"

Mr. Vega drove up to the gatehouse. Nobody was inside, but there was a sign.

Rotate the triangle clockwise 90° to enter.

Read·Think·Write Which way will the triangle point after it is rotated?

With a twinkle in his eye, Mr. Vega asked, "What should I do?"

Hector almost jumped out of his seat. "Turn it, Dad. When you rotate a figure, you turn it."

Mr. Vega reached out the car window and turned the triangle around once. The gates did not open.

"No, Dad," said Isabella. "The sign says to rotate it 90 degrees, so you only need to turn it a quarter of the way around." Isabella reached out the window and turned the triangle on its side, so the top was pointing to the right. The gate slid open.

With a cheer, the three drove through the gate and up the driveway. They got out of the car and stared at the enormous building in front of them.

The front door of the Acme Toy Company was gigantic. On either side of the door stood strange-looking plants. Each was about six feet tall with bright orange stems and purple leaves. Flowers the size of teacups poked through the leaves.

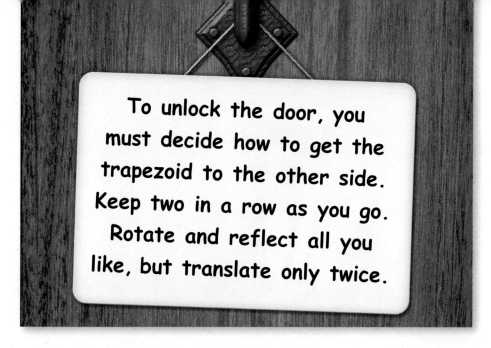

To unlock the door, you must decide how to get the trapezoid to the other side. Keep two in a row as you go. Rotate and reflect all you like, but translate only twice.

A sign hung from the doorknob.

"A riddle!" shouted Hector. "Look! Up there!"

On the left side of the door was a blue trapezoid. The word Lock was written on the door below it. On the right side, directly across from Lock, they found the word Unlock.

"We have to move that trapezoid to Unlock," said Isabella. "But how?"

"Rotate and reflect all you like," read Hector, "but translate only twice. Wait! I remember those words from math class."

Read·Think·Write How are Isabella and Hector allowed to move the trapezoid?

"Yes," agreed Isabella. "When you rotate a figure, you turn it around a point. And when you reflect, it's like flipping the figure over a line. What is translate?"

"When you translate a figure, you move it along a straight line," explained Hector.

"Well, we can only translate twice," said Isabella. She reached up and flipped the trapezoid down. "What if we reflect it this way?"

The other side of the trapezoid was red. As soon as Isabella let it go, a loud buzzer sounded and the trapezoid flipped itself back up. The Vegas all jumped.

"Well, I guess we can't do that!" said Mr. Vega.

"'Keep two in a row as you go,'" read Hector. "I wonder what that means." He tried to reflect the trapezoid up, showing the red side. Again, it buzzed at them and flipped itself back to the blue side.

"Maybe we have to keep the same color twice in a row," suggested Isabella. She rotated the trapezoid clockwise 90 degrees so that it was standing on one vertex. The buzzer did not buzz. The first blue trapezoid stayed where it was, and a second one appeared on the door.

Lock   Unlock

"All right!" cheered Hector. "It stayed! Let's try rotating it again."

"No. Keep two in a row as you go," said Isabella. "We already have two blues. Now we need a red."

Read·Think·Write How can Hector move the trapezoid so that the red side is showing?

Hector flipped the trapezoid down, showing the red side. The trapezoid buzzed and flipped back up.

Isabella giggled. "I guess that was the wrong way."

Hector tried again. He flipped the trapezoid to his right. A red trapezoid appeared on the door.

"This is fun!" laughed Hector. "Okay, we have to keep the red side showing. Should I try translating it?"

Isabella and Mr. Vega agreed that he should. Hector slid the trapezoid toward Unlock. This time, the red trapezoid spun, making a Gong! Gong! Gong! sound.

When the trapezoid stopped spinning, it was in the exact same place it had started.

"Let me try," said Isabella. She slid the red trapezoid straight down the door. As it moved, the figure made a sound like a bell ringing. Isabella let go and a new red trapezoid appeared directly below the first.

"Good job, Isabella," Mr. Vega said. "Now we have two reds in a row. What are you going to do next?"

"We need a blue one," said Isabella.

"Reflect! Reflect!" shouted Hector.

Isabella flipped the trapezoid to the right, and a new blue trapezoid appeared. "Okay, I'm going to try translating it again."

Isabella moved the blue trapezoid to the right. As soon as she let go, it buzzed and flew back to its original spot.

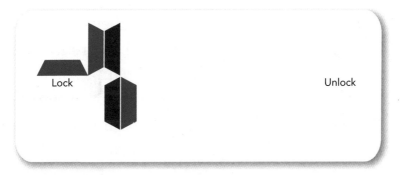

Read·Think·Write How else can Isabella move the trapezoid so that it stays on the blue side?

Isabella rotated the blue trapezoid 90 degrees clockwise. A new blue trapezoid appeared.

"That's two in a row," said Hector. He flipped the blue trapezoid to the right. Bells rang and a red trapezoid appeared on the door.

"We're getting closer," said Isabella, "but we need to get it back up toward Unlock."

Hector rotated the red trapezoid clockwise 90 degrees. Bells rang and a new red trapezoid appeared.

"We need two blues now," said Isabella.

Hector grabbed the red trapezoid and reflected it to the right. A blue trapezoid appeared.

"Let's try another translation," suggested Isabella.

Hector slid the blue trapezoid up until it was even with the word Unlock. Bells continued to ring.

"We're almost done," said Hector. "Let's reflect now." He flipped the trapezoid to the right.